The *Path of*
Peace

HENRI J. M. NOUWEN

The Path of Peace

CROSSROAD • NEW YORK

1995

The Crossroad Publishing Company
370 Lexington Avenue, New York, NY 10017

Copyright © 1995 by Henri J. M. Nouwen

Printed in the United States of America

ISBN 0-8245-2002-5

*H*OW TO SPEAK ABOUT PEACE? During the past years my own life has gone through so many changes that I have lost much of my self-confidence. A few years ago it seemed rather easy to get up in front of many people and give them some suggestions about how to be people of peace. I was able to do that with a certain ease and with the conviction that I had something important to say.

As I was preparing this short essay, however, I experienced a deep inner emptiness, a sense of futility in regard to words, even a despair about saying anything about peace, peacemaking, or a spirituality of peace. I was tempted to call it off. My poverty seemed too paralyzing.

But I am here and the reason is that I finally decided to share my poverty and trust that God does not want me to hide it from you. In the past I have often said that prayer, resistance, and community are the three core aspects of peace work. I still believe that this is true, but I question the value of saying it. Do these concepts generate what they express? I am no longer as sure as I was before. I am no longer sure of the use of any words in helping us to become the people God calls us to be.

So what to do now? After some agonizing hours of thinking about it all, I felt that I should tell you a little bit about my present life and try to discover there some aspect of the peace of Jesus we are searching for.

Some years ago I moved from Harvard to Daybreak, that is, from an institution for the best and the brightest to a community for mentally handicapped people. Daybreak, close to Toronto, is part of an international federation of communities called l'Arche — the Ark — where mentally handicapped men and women and their assistants try to live together in the spirit of the Beatitudes. I live in a house with six handicapped people and three other assistants. None of the assistants is specially trained to work with people with a mental handicap, but we receive all the help we need from doctors, psychiatrists, behavioral management people, social workers, and physiotherapists in town.

When there are no special crises, we live together as a family, gradually forgetting who is handicapped and who is not. We are simply John, Bill, Trevor, Raymond, Adam, Rose, Steve, Jane, Naomi, and Henri. We all have our gifts, our struggles, our strengths and weaknesses. We eat together, play together, pray together, and go out together. We all have our own preferences in terms of work, food, and movies, and we all have our problems in getting along with someone in the house, whether handicapped or not. We laugh a lot. We cry a lot too. Sometimes both at the same time.

Every morning when I say, "Good morning, Raymond," he says, "I am not awake yet. Saying good morning to everyone each day is unreal." Last Christmas Eve Trevor wrapped marsh-mallows in silver paper as peace gifts for everyone, and during the Christmas dinner he climbed on a chair, lifted his glass, and said, "Ladies and gentlemen, this is not a celebration, this is Christmas."

When one of the men speaking on the phone with someone was bothered by the cigarette smoke of an assistant, he yelled angrily, "Stop smoking! I can't hear." And every guest who comes for dinner is received by Bill with the question, "Hey, tell me, what is a turkey in suspense?" When the newcomer confesses ignorance, Bill, with a big grin on his face, says, "I will tell you tomorrow." And then he starts laughing so loudly that the visitor has to laugh with him whether he or she finds the joke funny or not so funny.

That is l'Arche; that is Daybreak; that is the family of ten I am living with day in and day out. What can life in this family of a few poor people reveal about the peace of Christ for which we are searching? Let me tell you the story of Adam, one of the ten people in our home, and let him become the silent spokesman of the peace that is not of this world.

Never having worked with handicapped people, I was not only apprehensive but even afraid to enter this unfamiliar world. This fear did not lessen when I was invited to work directly with Adam. Adam is the weakest person of our family. He is a twenty-five-year-old man who cannot speak, cannot dress or undress himself, cannot walk alone or eat without much help. He does not cry or laugh and only occasionally makes eye contact. His back is distorted and his arm and leg movements are very twisted. He suffers from severe epilepsy and, notwithstanding heavy medication, there are few days without "grand mal" seizures. Sometimes, as he grows suddenly rigid, he utters a howling groan, and on a few occasions I have seen a big tear coming down his cheek. It takes me about an hour and a half to wake Adam up, give him his medication, undress him, carry him into his bath, wash him, shave him, clean his teeth, dress him, walk him to the kitchen, give him his breakfast, put him in his wheelchair, and bring him to the place where he spends most of the day with various therapeutic exercises.

When a grand mal seizure occurs during this sequence of activities, much more time is needed, and often he has to return to sleep to regain some of the energy spent during such a seizure.

I tell you all of this not to give you a nursing report but to share with you something quite intimate. After a month of working this way with Adam, something started to happen to me that never had happened to me before. This deeply handicapped young man, who by many outsiders is considered an embarrassment, a distortion of humanity, a useless creature who should not have been allowed to be born, started to become my dearest companion. As my fears gradually decreased, a love started to emerge in me so full of tenderness and affection that most of my other tasks seemed boring and superficial compared with the hours spent with Adam. Out of this broken body and broken mind emerged a most beautiful human being offering me a greater gift than I would ever be able to offer him. It is hard for me to find adequate words for this experience, but somehow Adam revealed to me who he was and who I was and how we can love each other.

As I carried his naked body into the bathwater, made big waves to let the water run fast around his chest and neck, rubbed noses with him, and told him all sorts of stories about him and me, I knew that two friends were communicating far beyond the realm of thought or emotion. Deep speaks to deep, spirit speaks to spirit, heart speaks to heart. I started to realize that there was a mutuality of love not based on shared knowledge or shared feelings, but on shared humanity. The longer I stayed with Adam the more clearly I started to see him as my gentle teacher, teaching me what no book, school, or professor could have ever taught me.

Am I romanticizing, making something beautiful out of something ugly, projecting my hidden need to be a father on a deeply retarded person, spiritualizing what in essence is a shameful human condition that needs to be prevented at all cost? I am enough of a psychologically trained intellectual to raise these questions. Recently — during the writing of this story — Adam's parents came for a visit. I asked them: "Tell me, during all the years you had Adam in your home, what did he give you?" His father smiled and said without a moment of hesitation: "He brought us peace . . . he is our peacemaker . . . our son of peace."

Let me, then, tell you about Adam's peace, a peace that the world cannot give. I am moved by the simple fact that probably the most important task I have is to give words to the peace of one who has no words. The gift of peace hidden in Adam's utter weakness is a gift not of the world, but certainly for the world. For this gift to become known, someone has to lift it up and hand it on. That, maybe, is the deepest meaning of being an assistant to handicapped people. It is helping them to share their gifts. Adam's gift of peace is rooted in *being* and in the *heart* and always calls forth *community*. Let me explore a little these three aspects of Adam's peace.

Rooted in Being

Adam's peace is first of all a peace rooted in *being*. How simple a truth, but how hard to live! Being is more important than doing. Adam can do nothing. He is completely dependent on others every moment of his life. His gift is his pure *being with us*. Every evening when I run home to "do" Adam — that means help him with his supper and put him to bed — I realize that the best thing I can do for Adam is to be with him. If Adam wants anything, it is that you be with him. And indeed that is the great joy: paying total attention to his breathing, his eating, his careful steps, looking at how he tries to lift a spoon to his mouth, or raises his left arm a little to make it easier for you to take off his shirt; always wondering about possible pains that he cannot express, but that still ask for relief.

Most of my past life has been built around the idea that my value depends on what I do. I made it through grade school, high school, and university. I earned my degrees and awards and I made my career. Yes, with many others I fought my way up to the lonely top of a little success, a little popularity, and a little power. But as I sit beside the slow and heavily breathing Adam, I start seeing how violent that journey was. So filled with desires to be better than others, so marked by rivalry and competition, so pervaded with compulsions and obsessions, and so spotted with moments of suspicion, jealousy, resentment, and revenge. Oh, sure, most of what I did was called ministry, the ministry of justice and peace, the ministry of forgiveness and reconciliation, the ministry of healing and wholeness. But when those who want peace are as interested in success, popularity, and power as those who want war, what then is the real difference between war and peace? When the peace is as much of this world as the war, what other choice is there but the choice between a war which we euphemistically call pacification and a peace in which the peacemakers violate one another's deepest values?

In his silent way Adam says to me, "Peace is first of all the art of being." I know he is right because after four months of being with Adam I am discovering in myself the beginning of an inner at-homeness that I didn't know before. I even feel the unusual desire to do a lot less and be a lot more, preferably with Adam.

As I cover him with his sheets and blankets and turn out the lights, I pray with Adam. He is always very quiet as if he knows that my praying voice sounds a little different from my speaking voice. I whisper in his ear: "May

all the angels protect you," and often he looks up at me from his pillow
and seems to know what I am talking
about. Since I began to pray with Adam
I have come to know better than before
that praying is being with Jesus and
simply spending time with him. Adam
keeps teaching me that.

Rooted in the Heart

Adam's peace is not only a peace rooted
in being, but also a peace rooted in the
heart. That true peace belongs to the
heart is such a radical statement that
only people as handicapped as Adam
seem to be able to get it across! Somehow during the centuries we have come
to believe that what makes us human

is our minds. Many people who do not know any Latin still seem to know the definition of a human being as a reasoning animal: *rationale animal est homo* (Seneca).

But Adam keeps telling me over and over again that what makes us human is not our minds but our hearts, not our ability to think but our ability to love. Whoever speaks about Adam as an animal-like creature misses the sacred mystery that Adam is fully capable of receiving and giving love. He is fully human, not a little bit human, not half human, not nearly human, but fully, completely human because he is all heart. And it is our heart that is made in the image and likeness of God. If this were not the case, how could I

ever say to you that Adam and I love
each other? How could I ever experience new life from simply being with
him? How could I ever believe that
moving away from teaching many men
and women to being taught by Adam is
a real step forward? I am speaking here
about something very, very real. It is the
primacy of the heart.

Let me say here that by heart I do
not mean the seat of human emotions
in contrast to the mind as the seat of
human thought. No, by heart I mean
the center of our being where God has
hidden the divine gifts of trust, hope,
and love. The mind tries to understand,
grasp problems, discern different aspects of reality, and probe the mysteries
of life. The heart allows us to enter

into relationships and become sons and daughters of God and brothers and sisters of each other. Long before our mind is able to exercise its power, our heart is already able to develop a trusting human relationship. I am convinced that this trusting human relationship even precedes the moment of our birth.

Here we are touching the origin of the spiritual life. Often people think that the spiritual life is the latest in coming and follows the development of the biological, emotional, and intellectual life. But living with Adam and reflecting on my experience with him makes me realize that God's loving spirit has touched us long before we can walk, feel, or talk. The spiritual life is given to us from the moment of our conception. It is the divine gift of love that makes the human person able to reveal a presence much greater than himself or herself.

When I say that I believe deeply that Adam can give and receive love and that there is a true mutuality between us, I do not make a naive psychological statement overlooking his severe handicaps. I am speaking about a love between us that transcends all thoughts and feelings precisely because it is rooted in God's first love, a love that precedes all human loves. The mystery of Adam is that in his deep mental and emotional brokenness he has become so empty of all human pride that he has become the preferable mediator of that first love. Maybe this will help you see why Adam is giving me a whole new understanding of God's love for the poor and the oppressed. He has offered me a new perspective on the well-known "preferential option" for the poor.

The peace that flows from Adam's broken heart is not of this world. It is not the result of political analysis, roundtable debates, discernment of the signs of the times, or well-thought-out strategies. All these activities of the mind have their role to play in the complex process of peacemaking. But they all will become easily perverted to a new way of warmaking if they are not put into the service of the divine peace that flows from the heart of those who are called the poor in spirit.

Calling Forth Community

The third and most tangible quality
of Adam's peace is that, while rooted
more in being than in doing and more
in the heart than in the mind, it is a
peace that always calls forth community. The most impressive aspect of my
life at l'Arche is that the handicapped
people hold us together as a family
and that the most handicapped people
are the true center of gravity of our
togetherness. Adam in his total vulnerability calls us together as a family. And
in fact, from the perspective of community formation, he turns everything
upside down. The weakest members
are the assistants. We come from different countries — Brazil, the United

States, Canada, and Holland — and our commitments are ambiguous at best. Some stay longer than others, but most move on after one or two years. Closer to the center are Raymond, Bill, John, and Trevor, who are relatively independent but still need much help and attention. They are permanent members of the family. They are with us for life and they keep us honest. Because of them conflicts never last very long, tensions are talked out, and disagreements resolved. But in the heart of our community are Rose and Adam, both deeply handicapped, and the weaker of the two is Adam.

Adam is the weakest of us all, but without any doubt the strongest bond among us all. Because of Adam there is always someone home; because of Adam there is a quiet rhythm in the house; because of Adam there are moments of silence and quiet; because of Adam there are always words of affection, gentleness, and tenderness; because of Adam there is patience and endurance; because of Adam there are smiles and tears visible to all; because of Adam there is always space for mutual forgiveness and healing ... yes, because of Adam there is peace among us. How otherwise could people from such different nationalities and cultures, people with such different characters and with such an odd variety of handicaps, whether mental or not, live together in peace?

Adam truly calls us together around

him and molds this motley group of strangers into a family. Adam is our true peacemaker. How mysterious are the ways of God: "God chose those who by human standards are fools to shame the wise; he chose those who by human standards are weak in order to shame the strong, those who by human standards are common and contemptible — indeed who count for nothing — to reduce to nothing all those who do count for something, so that no human being might feel boastful before God" (1 Cor. 1:27–30). Adam gives flesh to these words of Paul. He teaches me the true mystery of community.

Most of my adult life I have tried to show the world that I could do it on my

"God chose those who by human standards are fools to shame the wise."

(1 Cor. 1:27)

own, that I needed others only to get me back on my lonely road. Those who have helped me helped me to become a strong, independent, self-motivated, creative man who would be able to survive in the long search for individual freedom. With many others, I wanted to become a self-sufficient star. And most of my fellow intellectuals joined me in that desire.

But all of us highly trained individuals are facing today a world on the brink of total destruction. And now we start to wonder how we might join forces to make peace! What kind of peace can this possibly be? Who can paint a portrait of people who all want to take the center seat? Who can build a beautiful church with people who are interested only in erecting the tower? Who can bake a birthday cake with people who want only to put the candles on? You all know the problem. When all want the honor of being the final peacemaker, there never will be peace.

Adam needs many people and nobody can boast of anything. Adam will never be "cured." His constant seizures even make it likely that medically things will only get worse. There are no successes to claim, and everyone who works with him does only a little bit. My part in his life is very, very small. Some cook for him, others do his laundry, some give him massages, others play music for him, take him for a walk, a swim, or a ride. Some look af-

33

ter his blood pressure and regulate his medicine; others look after his teeth.

Although with all this assistance Adam doesn't change and often seems to slip away in a state of total exhaustion, a community of peace has emerged around him. It is a community that certainly does not want to put its light under a basket, because the peace community that Adam has called forth is not there just for Adam, but for all who belong to Adam's race. It is a community that proclaims that God has chosen to descend among us in complete weakness and vulnerability and thus to reveal to us the glory of God.

Thus, as you see, Adam is gradually teaching me something about the peace that is not of this world. It is a peace not constructed by tough competition, hard thinking, and individual stardom, but rooted in simply being present to each other, a peace that speaks about the first love of God by which we are all held and a peace that keeps calling us to community, a fellowship of the weak. Adam has never said a word to me. He will never do so. But every night as I put him to bed I say "thank you" to him. How much closer can one come to the Word that became flesh and dwells among us?

I have told you about Adam and about Adam's peace. But you are not part of l'Arche, you do not live at Daybreak, you are not a member of Adam's family. Like me, however, you search for peace and want to find peace in your heart, your family, and your world. But looking around us in the world, we see concentration camps and refugee camps; we see overcrowded prisons; we see the burning of villages, genocidal actions, kidnappings, torture, and murder; we see starving children, neglected elderly, and countless men and women without food, shelter, or a job. We see people sleeping in the city streets, young girls and boys selling themselves for others' pleasure; we see violence and rape and the desperation of millions of fearful and lonely people.

Seeing all this, we realize that there is no peace in our world. And still... that is what our hearts desire most. You and I may have tried giving money, demonstrating, overseas projects, and many other things — but as we grow older we are faced with the fact that the peace we waited for still has not come. Something in us is in danger of growing cold, bitter, and resentful, and we are tempted to withdraw from it all and limit ourselves to the easier task of personal survival. But that is a demonic temptation.

I have told you about Adam and his peace to offer you a quiet guide with a gentle heart who gives you a little light to walk with through this dark world. Adam does not solve anything. Even with all the support he receives, he cannot change his own utter poverty. As he grows older, he grows poorer and poorer and poorer. A little infection, an unhappy fall, an accidental swallowing of his own tongue during a seizure, and many other small incidents may take him suddenly away from us. When he dies, nobody will be able to boast about anything.

And still, what a light he brings! In Adam's name I therefore say to you: Do not give up working for peace. But always remember that the peace for which you work is not of this world. Do not let yourself be distracted by the great noises of war, the dramatic descriptions of misery, and the sensational expressions of human cruelty. The newspapers, movies, and war novels may make you numb, but they do not create in you a true desire for peace. They tend to create feelings of shame, guilt, and powerlessness, and these feelings are the worst motives for peace work.

Keep your eyes on the prince of peace, the one who doesn't cling to his divine power; the one who refuses to turn stones into bread, jump from great heights, and rule with great power; the one who says, "Blessed are the poor, the gentle, those who mourn, and those who hunger and thirst for righteousness; blessed are the merciful, the pure in heart, the peacemakers and those who are persecuted in the cause of up-rightness" (see Matt. 5:3–11); the one who touches the lame, the crippled, and the blind; the one who speaks words of forgiveness and encouragement; the one who dies alone, rejected, and de-spised. Keep your eyes on him who becomes poor with the poor, weak with the weak, and who is rejected with the rejected. He is the source of all peace.

Where is this peace to be found? The answer is clear. In weakness. First of all, in our own weakness, in those places of our hearts where we feel most broken, most insecure, most in agony, most afraid. Why there? Because there our familiar ways of controlling our world are being stripped away; there we are called to let go from doing much, thinking much, and relying on our self-sufficiency. Right there where we are weakest the peace that is not of this world is hidden.

In Adam's name I say to you: Claim that peace that remains unknown to so many and make it your own. Because with that peace in your heart you will have new eyes to see and new ears to hear and gradually recognize that same peace in places you would have least expected.

Not long ago I was in Honduras. It was my first time in Central America since I had come to Daybreak and become friends with Adam. I suddenly realized that I was a little less consumed by anger about the political manipulations, a little less distracted by the blatant injustices, and a little less paralyzed by the realization that the future of Honduras looks very dark. Visiting the severely handicapped Raphael in the l'Arche community near Tegucigalpa, I saw the same peace I had seen in Adam, and hearing many stories about the gifts of joy offered by the poorest of the poor to the oh-so-serious assistants who came from France, Belgium, the United States, and Canada, I knew that peace is the gift of God often hidden from the wise and wealthy and revealed to the inarticulate and poor.

I am not saying that the questions about peace in Bosnia, Haiti, and Rwanda are no longer important. Far from that. I am only saying that the seeds of national and international peace are already sown in the soil of our own suffering and the suffering of the poor, and that we truly can trust that these seeds, like the mustard seeds of the gospel, will produce large shrubs in which many birds can find a place to rest.

As long as we think and live as if there is no peace yet and that it all is going to depend on ourselves to make it come about, we are on the road to self-destruction. But when we trust that the God of love has already given the peace we are searching for, we will see this peace breaking through the broken soil of our human condition and we will be able to let it grow fast and even heal the economic and political maladies of our time. With this trust in our hearts, we will be able to hear the words: "Blessed are the peacemakers, for they shall inherit the earth." It fills me with a special joy that all the Adams of this world will be the first to receive this inheritance.

Conclusion

It is time to end. Somehow it feels hard to end. There are so many unspoken words, unexpressed feelings, and unrevealed mysteries. But I have to trust that you will know about them even when they have remained hidden. . . .

Many people live in the night; a few live in the day. We all know about night and day, darkness and light. We know about it in our hearts; we know about it in our families and communities; we know about it in our world. The peace that the world does not give is the light that dispels the darkness. Every bit of that peace makes the day come!

Let me conclude with an old Hasidic tale that summarizes much of what I have tried to say.

The rabbi asked his students: "How can we determine the hour of dawn, when the night ends and the day begins?"

One of the rabbi's students suggested: "When from a distance you can distinguish between a dog and a sheep?"

"No," was the answer of the rabbi.

"Is it when one can distinguish between a fig tree and a grapevine?" asked a second student.

"No," the rabbi said.

"Please tell us the answer, then," said the students.

"It is, then," said the wise teacher, "when you can look into the face of human beings and you have enough light [in you] to recognize them as your brothers and sisters. Up until then it is night, and darkness is still with us."

Let us pray for the light. It is the peace the world cannot give.

HENRI J. M. NOUWEN, author of more than thirty books, including *The Return of the Prodigal Son, Life of the Beloved, In the Name of Jesus,* and *Our Greatest Gift,* has taught at the University of Notre Dame, Yale, and Harvard. For the last seven years, he has shared his life with people with mental handicaps, as pastor of the l'Arche Daybreak community in Toronto, Canada.

Other books in *The Path* series